DISNEY CLASSIC SONGS

ISBN-13: 978-1-4234-1277-X
ISBN-10: 1-4234-1277-9

Wonderland Music Company, Inc.

Walt Disney Music Company

HAL•LEONARD®
CORPORATION

7777 W. BLUEMOUND RD. P.O. BOX 13819 MILWAUKEE, WI 53213

The following songs are the property of:
Bourne Co.
Music Publishers
5 West 37th Street
New York, NY 10018

WHEN I SEE AN ELEPHANT FLY
WHEN YOU WISH UPON A STAR
WITH A SMILE AND A SONG

Visit Hal Leonard Online at **www.halleonard.com**

ON THE CD . . .

Julian Brightman
Julian has sung from Broadway to the White House, and all points in between. Career highlights include *Peter Pan* and *Hello, Dolly!* on Broadway; *West Side Story* at the legendary La Scala Opera House in Milan; and *The Fantasticks* at Washington, D.C.'s historic Ford's Theatre.

Sarah Jane Everman
Sarah has appeared at the New York City Center with the Encores series. She has performed on Broadway in *Wicked, Wonderful Town*, and *The Apple Tree*.

Susan Derry
Susan has performed on Broadway in *Wonderful Town* (Eileen) and *The Phantom of the Opera* (Christine); and she has appeared as a guest soloist with the New York Pops at Carnegie Hall. She attended Northwestern University and received her Masters in Voice from the Manhattan School of Music.

Jeff Whiting
Jeff has originated numerous roles for Walt Disney Entertainment, including Quasimodo in Disneyworld's *Hunchback of Notre Dame*, and Peter Pan and Young Hercules aboard the Disney Magic, as a member of the original cast of the Disney Cruise Line's inaugural season. Jeff currently serves as Assistant Director to the National Tours of *Hairspray* and *The Producers*.

Producer **Michael Dansicker** has worked as arranger, composer, musical director and pianist on over 100 Broadway and Off-Broadway productions; from *Grease* (1975) to *Series of Dreams* (Tharp/Dylan Project '05.) His musical *Twenty Fingers, Twenty Toes* (Book, Music and Lyrics) has been performed Off-Broadway at the NY WPA Theatre and The York and his Boogie-Woogie Opera *Swing Shift* was performed at the Manhattan Theatre Club. He has composed original music for over a dozen plays in New York, including The *Glass Menagerie* (revival with Jessica Tandy) and *Total Abandon* (with Richard Dreyfus), and musically supervised the Royal Shakespeare Company transfers of *Piaf, Good*, and *Les Liasons Dangereuses*. He served as vocal consultant to the hit films *Elf* (New Line Cinema), *Analyze That!* (Warner Bros.), and *Meet the Parents* (Universal), and also scored the dance sequences for Paramount's comedy classic *Brain Donors* (starring John Turturro). In the world of concert dance, he has composed and scored pieces for Twyla Tharp, American Ballet Theatre, Geoffrey Holder, Mikhail Baryshnikov, and The Joffrey, as well as serving as pianist to Jerome Robbins and Agnes Demille. Michael currently works as creative consultant to Walt Disney Entertainment. For Hal Leonard Corporation, he composed the music for *The Audition Suite* (lyrics by Martin Charnin) and compiled the four books of The *16-Bar Theatre Audition* series. As a vocal coach, he works with the top talent in New York and Hollywood (including Sony's pop division). As audition pianist, he works regularly with important casting directors on both coasts, and for 15 years has played all major auditions for Jay Binder, the "dean" of Broadway casting. Mr. Dansicker's original music is licensed by BMI. He holds a MA from the Catholic University of America.

CONTENTS

Page			Vocal Track	Accompaniment Track
4	The Bare Necessities	*The Jungle Book*	1	11
10	Candle on the Water	*Pete's Dragon*	2	12
13	A Dream Is a Wish Your Heart Makes	*Cinderella*	3	13
16	The Lord Is Good to Me	*Melody Time*	4	14
20	The Second Star to the Right	*Peter Pan*	5	15
23	So This Is Love (The Cinderella Waltz)	*Cinderella*	6	16
26	When I See an Elephant Fly	*Dumbo*	7	17
32	When You Wish Upon a Star	*Pinocchio*	8	18
29	With a Smile and a Song	*Snow White and the Seven Dwarfs*	9	19
36	Zip-A-Dee-Doo-Dah	*Song of the South*	10	20

Singers on the CD:
Julian Brightman (tracks 1, 5, 7, 8, 10), **Sarah Jane Everman** (tracks 3, 6),
Susan Derry (tracks 2, 9), **Jeff Whiting** (track 4)

Pianists on the CD:
Ruben Piirainen (1, 4, 10, 11, 14, 20), Hank Powell (2, 3, 5-9, 12, 13, 15-19)

Vocal Tracks produced by Michael Dansicker
Engineered by Chip Fabrizi at P.P.I. Recording, Inc., New York City

THE BARE NECESSITIES
from Walt Disney's *The Jungle Book*

Words and Music by
Terry Gilkyson

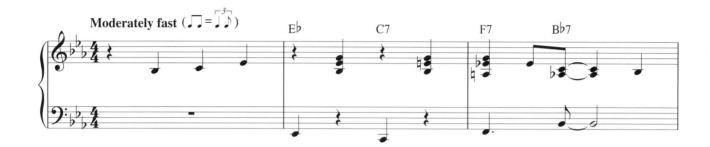

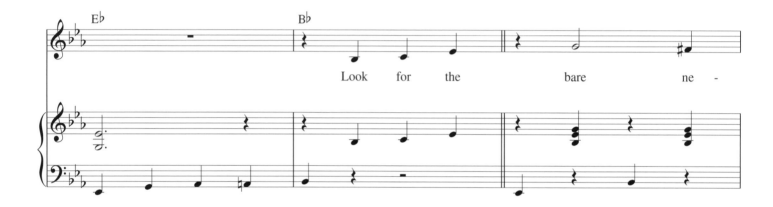

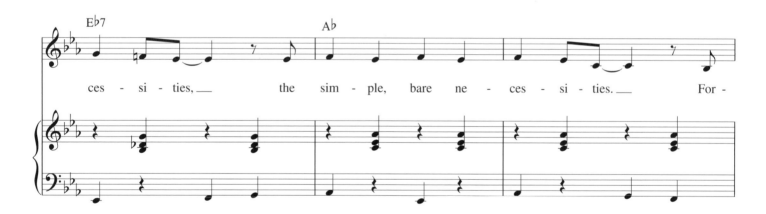

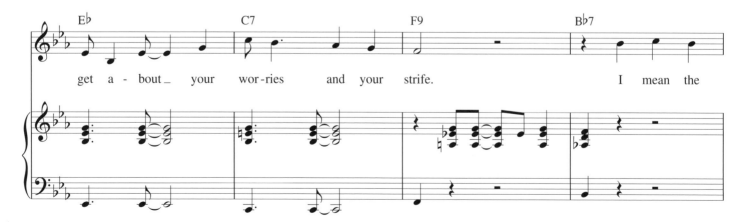

bare ne - ces - si - ties, ___ oh, Moth - er Na - ture's

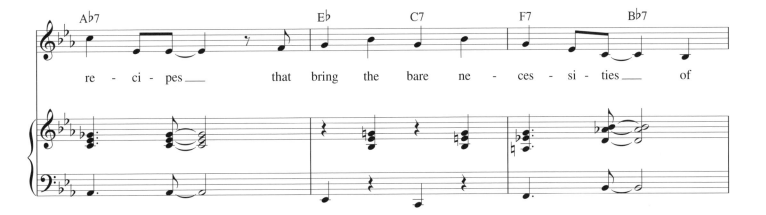

re - ci - pes ___ that bring the bare ne - ces - si - ties ___ of

life.

Wher - ev - er I wan - der, ___
When you pick ___ a paw - paw ___

wher - ev - er I roam,
or a prick - ly pear

I could - n't be
and you ___ pick a

fond - er _____ of my big home.
raw paw, _____ well, next time, be - ware.

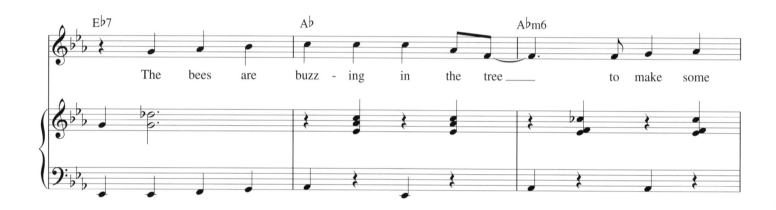

The bees are buzz - ing in the tree _____ to make some

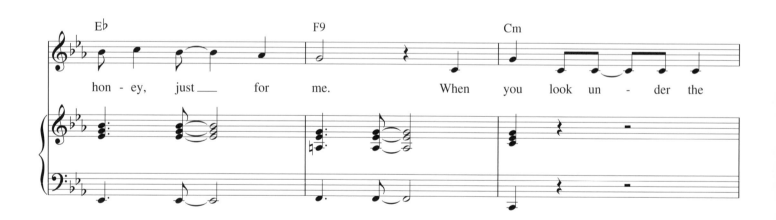

hon - ey, just _____ for me. When you look un - der the

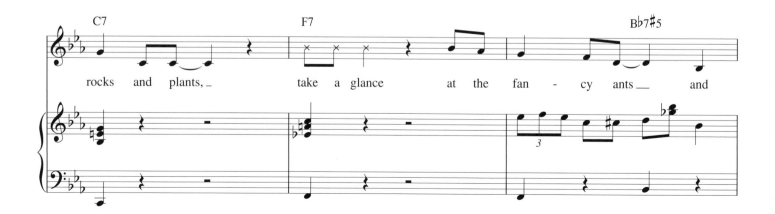

rocks and plants, _____ take a glance at the fan - cy ants _____ and

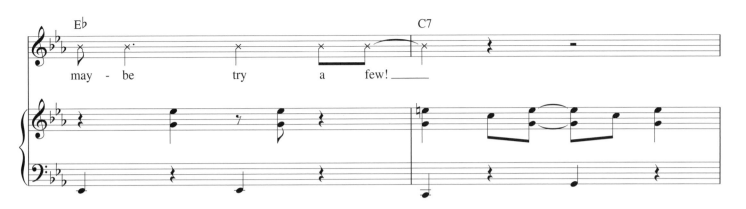

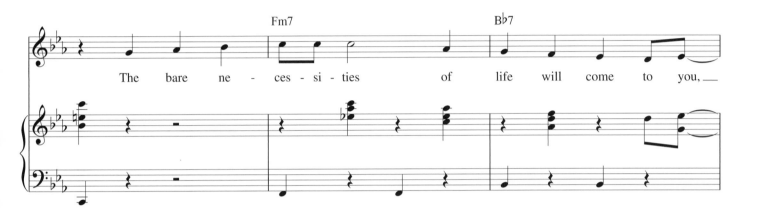

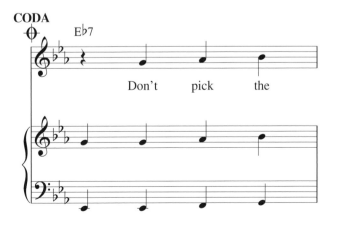

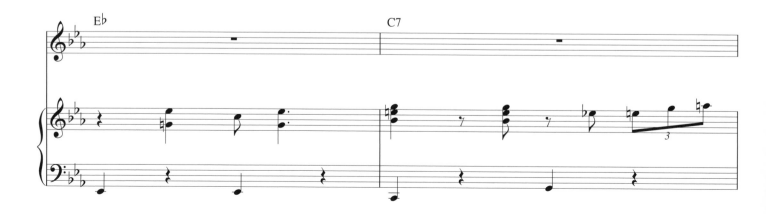

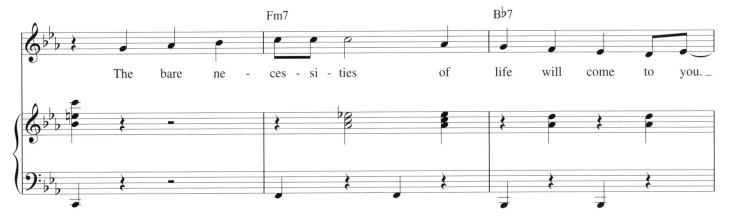

The bare ne - ces - si - ties of life will come to you. _

They'll come to you. _____

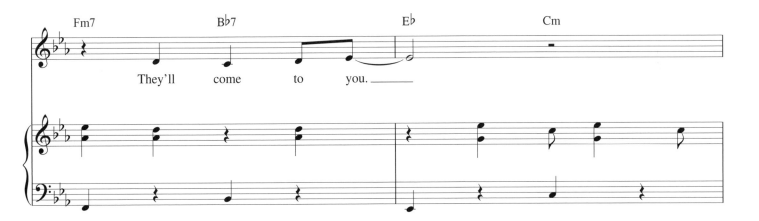

They'll come to you. _____

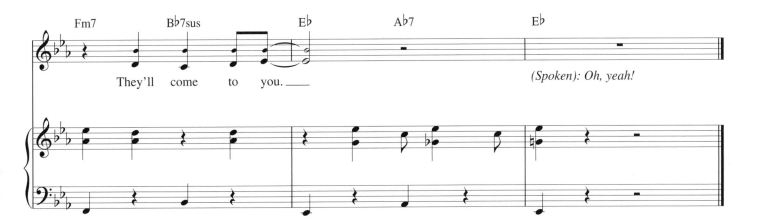

They'll come to you. _____

(Spoken): Oh, yeah!

CANDLE ON THE WATER
from Walt Disney's *Pete's Dragon*

Words and Music by Al Kasha
and Joel Hirschhorn

Smoothly

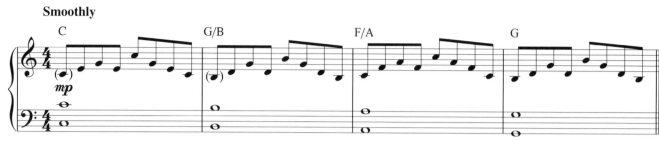

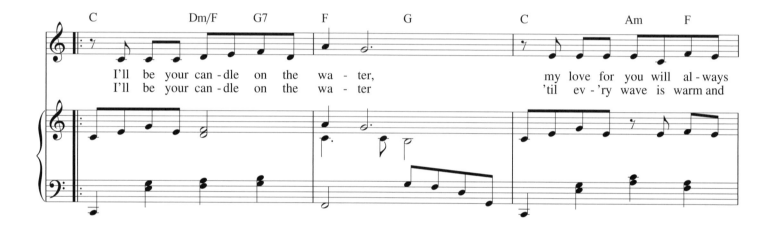

I'll be your can - dle on the wa - ter, my love for you will al - ways
I'll be your can - dle on the wa - ter 'til ev - 'ry wave is warm and

burn. I know you're lost and drift - ing, but the clouds are lift - ing.
bright. My soul is there be - side you, let this can - dle guide you;

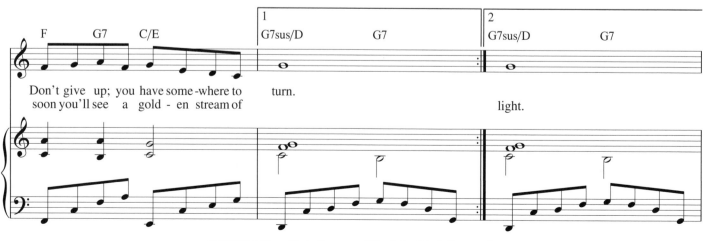

Don't give up; you have some - where to turn.
soon you'll see a gold - en stream of light.

A cold and friend-less tide has found you, don't let the storm - y dark-ness

pull you down. I'll paint a ray of hope a - round you,

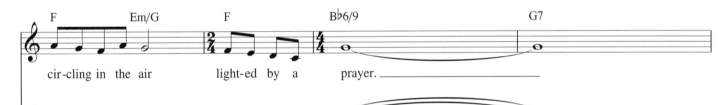

cir-cling in the air light-ed by a prayer.

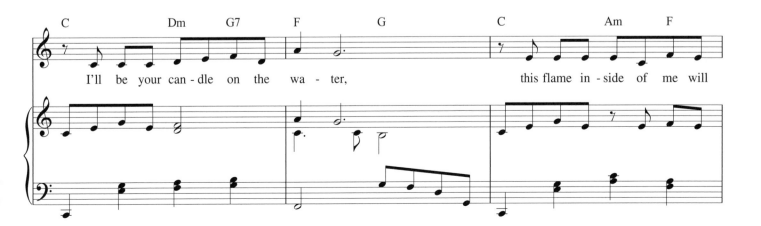

I'll be your can - dle on the wa - ter, this flame in - side of me will

grow. Keep hold-ing on, you'll make it, here's my hand so take it.

Look for me reach-ing out to show as sure as riv-ers flow, I'll nev er let you

go, I'll nev er let you go, I'll nev er let you

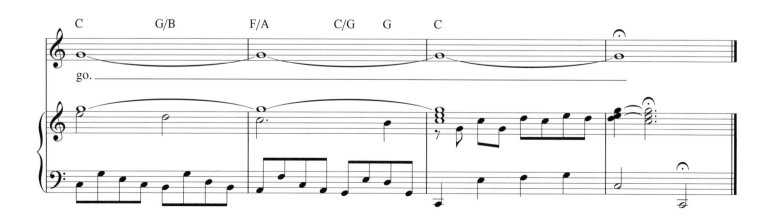

go. _____

A DREAM IS A WISH
YOUR HEART MAKES

from Walt Disney's *Cinderella*

Words and Music by Mack David,
Al Hoffman and Jerry Livingston

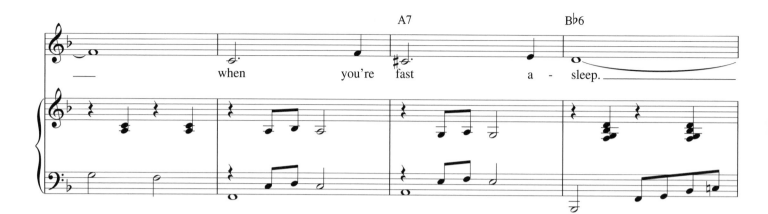

when you're fast a - sleep._____

In dreams you will lose your heart - aches;_____

what - ev - er you wish for you keep._____

Have faith in your dreams and some - day_____

your rain-bow will come smil - ing through

no mat - ter how your heart is griev - ing if you keep on be -

liev - ing the dream that you wish will come true.

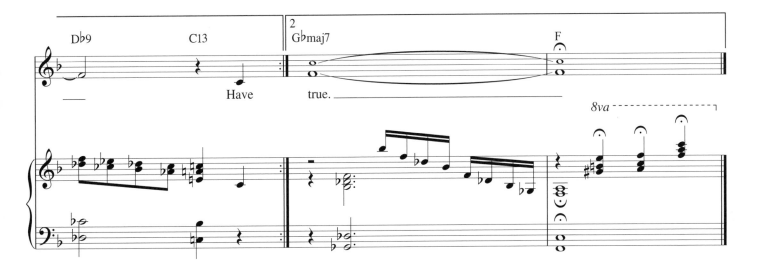

Have true.

THE LORD IS GOOD TO ME

from Walt Disney's *Melody Time*

Words and Music by Kim Gannon
and Walter Kent

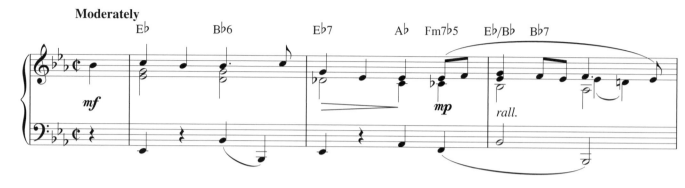

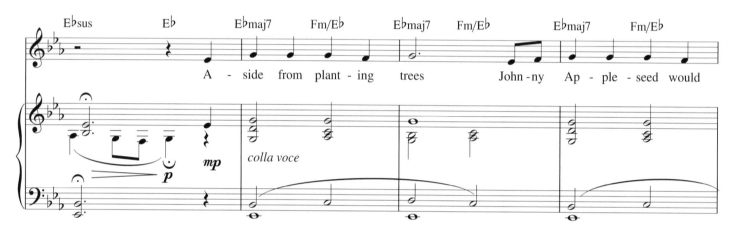

A - side from plant - ing trees John - ny Ap - ple - seed would

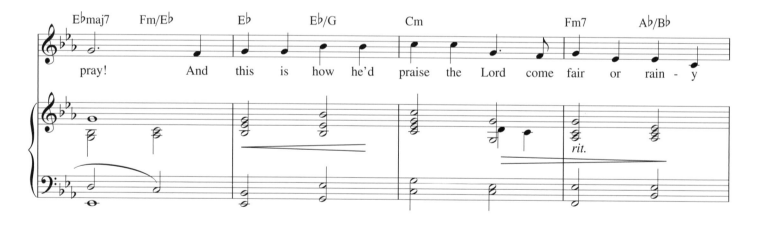

pray! And this is how he'd praise the Lord come fair or rain - y

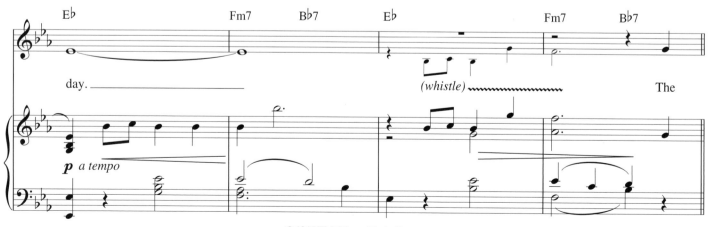

day. _____ (whistle) ~~~~~~~~~~ The

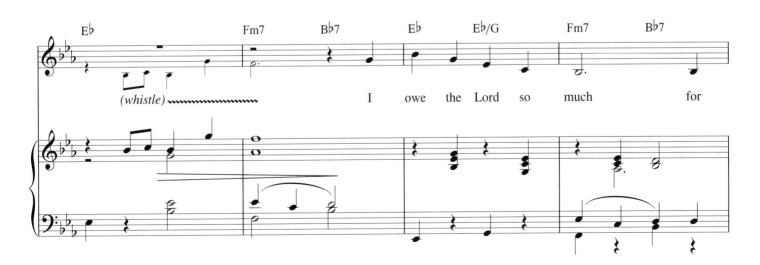

ev - 'ry -thing I see. I'm cer - tain if it weren't for Him there'd

be no ap - ples on this limb, yes, He's been good to

me. _____ Oh here am I 'neath a blue, blue sky a -

do - in' as I please, sing - in' with my feath -ered friends, _

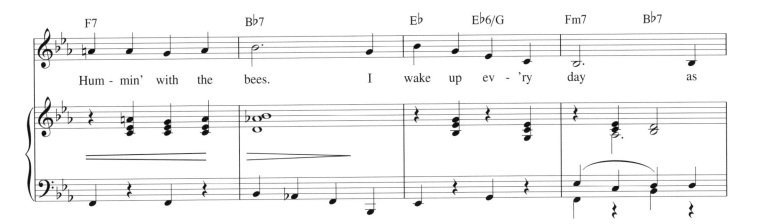

Hum - min' with the bees. I wake up ev - 'ry day as

hap - py as can be be - cause I know that with His care my

ap - ple trees they will still be there, Oh the Lord's been good to

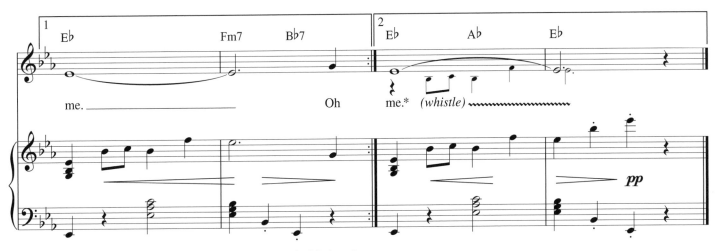

me. _____ Oh me.* *(whistle)* ~~~~~~~~

*The singer may choose to leave off the last "me" and whistle only.

THE SECOND STAR TO THE RIGHT
from Walt Disney's *Peter Pan*

Words by Sammy Cahn
Music by Sammy Fain

rare; and if it's Nev - er - land you need, its

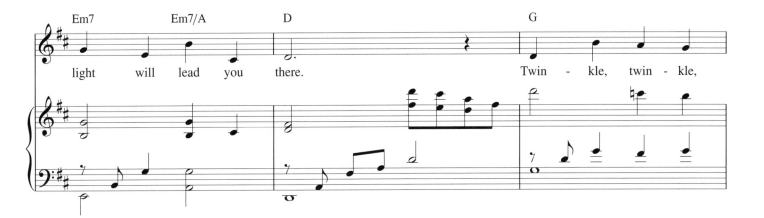

light will lead you there. Twin - kle, twin - kle,

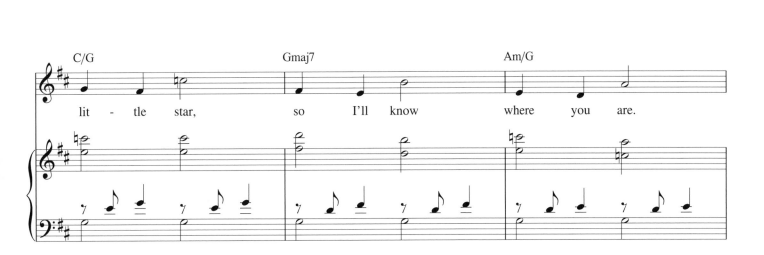

lit - tle star, so I'll know where you are.

Gleam - ing in the skies a - bove, lead me to the

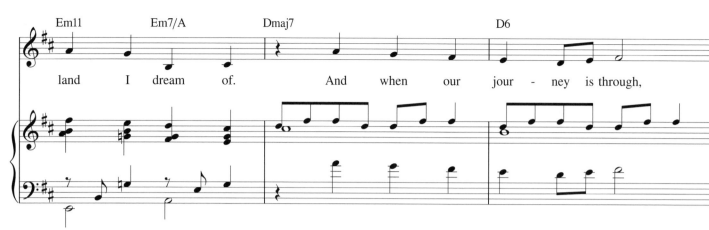

land I dream of. And when our jour - ney is through,

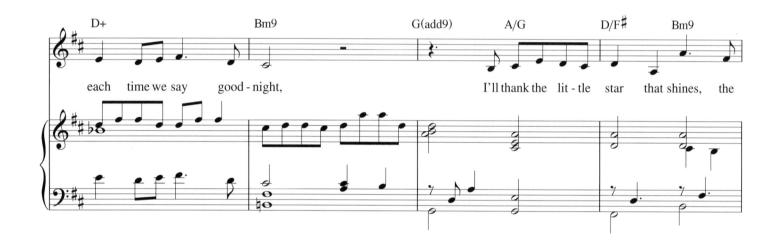

each time we say good - night, I'll thank the lit - tle star that shines, the

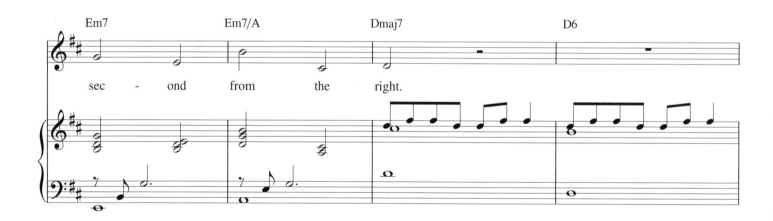

sec - ond from the right.

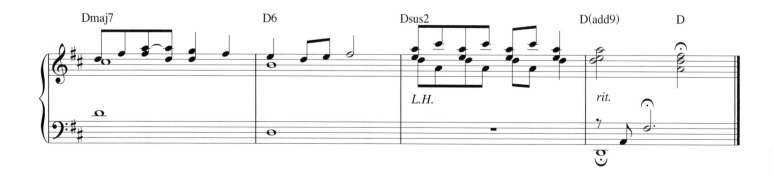

SO THIS IS LOVE
(The Cinderella Waltz)
from Walt Disney's *Cinderella*

Words and Music by Mack David,
Al Hoffman and Jerry Livingston

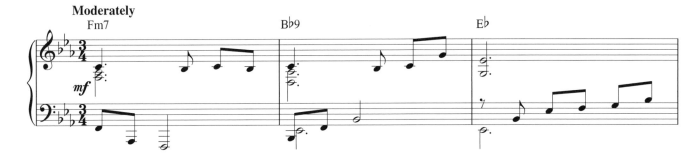

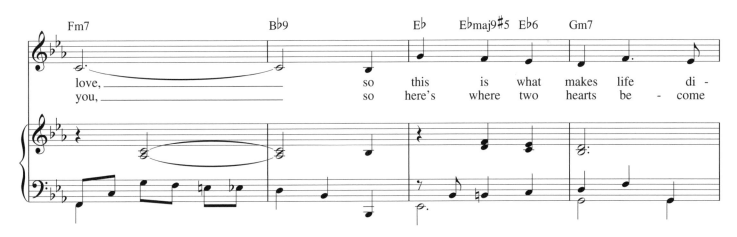

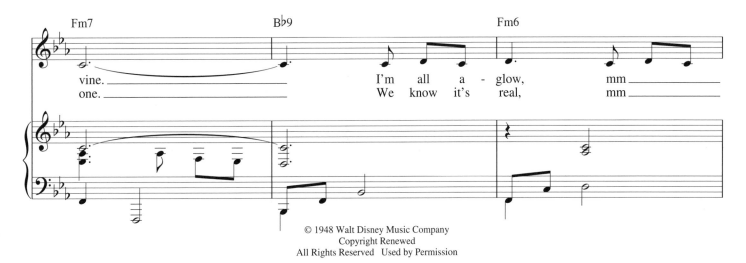

and now I know _____ the key to all
and yes, it's true _____ our love has

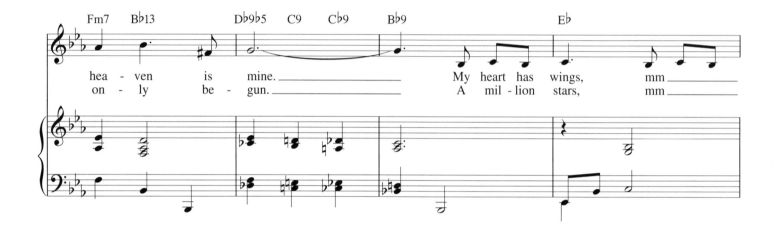

hea - ven is mine. _____ My heart has wings, mm _____
on - ly be - gun. _____ A mil - lion stars, mm _____

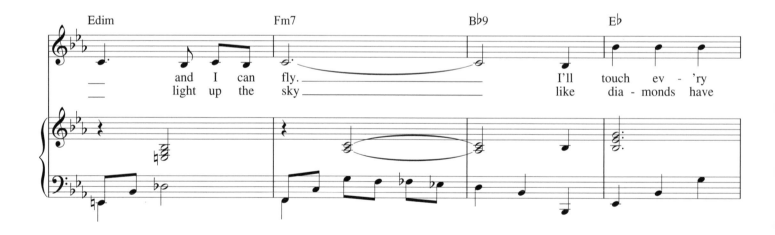

___ and I can fly. _____ I'll touch ev - 'ry
light up the sky _____ like dia - monds have

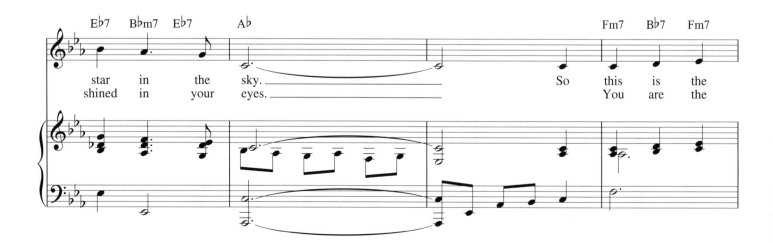

star in the sky. _____ So this is the
shined in your eyes. _____ You are the

WHEN I SEE AN ELEPHANT FLY
from Walt Disney's *Dumbo*

Words by Ned Washington
Music by Oliver Wallace

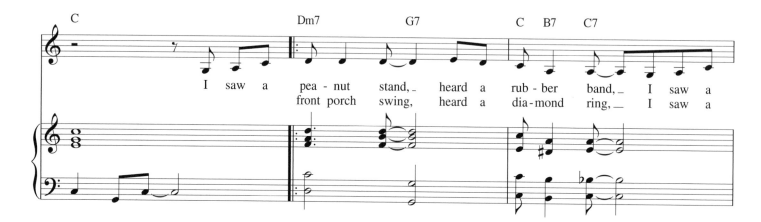

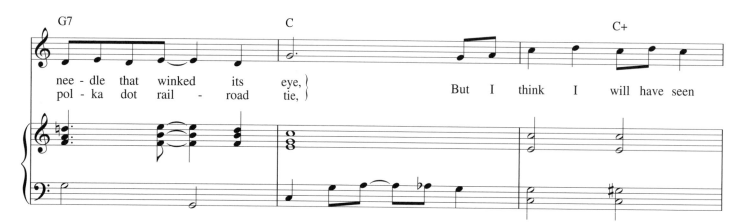

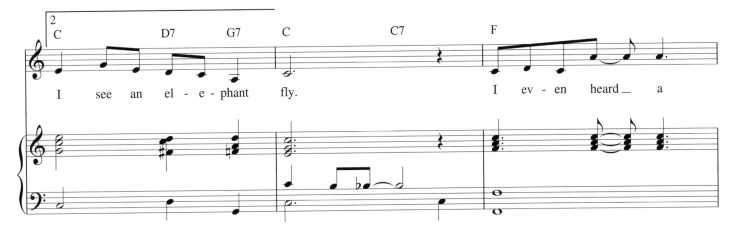

I see an el - e - phant fly. I ev - en heard _ a

choc - o - late drop, _ I went in - to a store, saw a bi - cy - cle shop. _

You can't de - ny _ the things that you see, _ But I know there's cer - tain things that

just can't be. _ The oth - er day by chance, _ saw an old barn dance, _ And I just

laugh'd till I thought I'd die But I think I will have seen

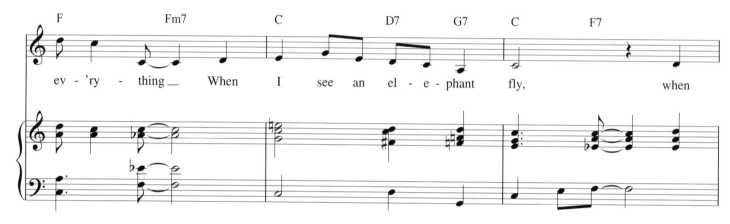

ev - 'ry - thing When I see an el - e - phant fly, when

I see an el - e - phant fly, when I see an

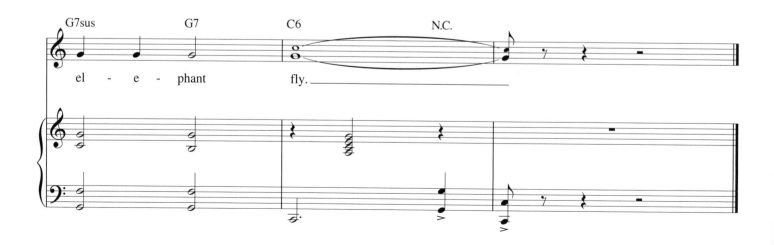

el - e - phant fly.

WITH A SMILE AND A SONG
from Walt Disney's *Snow White and the Seven Dwarfs*

Words by Larry Morey
Music by Frank Churchill

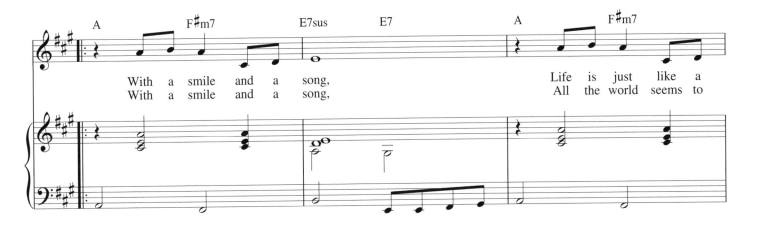

With a smile and a song,   Life is just like a
With a smile and a song,   All the world seems to

bright sun-ny day,   Your cares fade a - way,____   And your heart is
wak - en a-new,   Re - joic - ing with you,____   As the song is

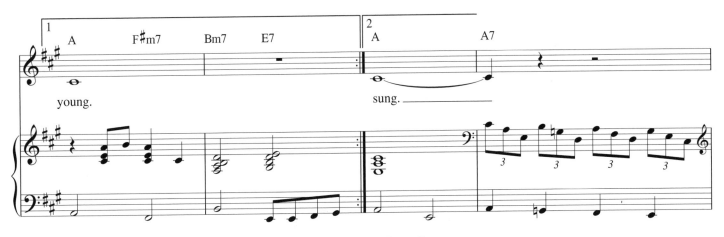

young.
sung.____

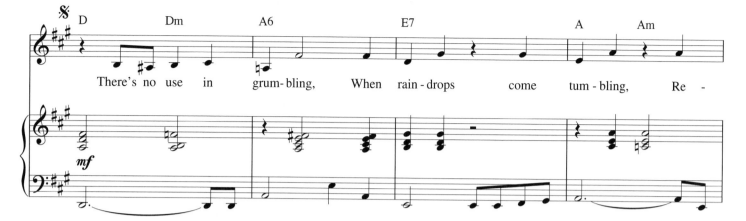

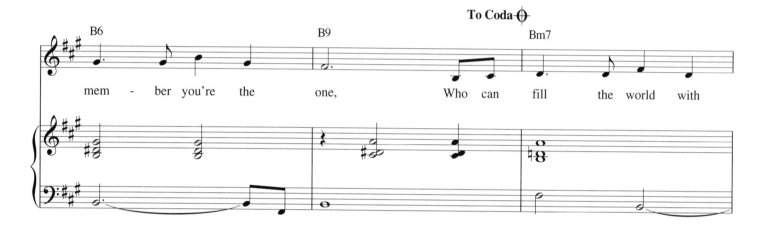

D.S. al Coda

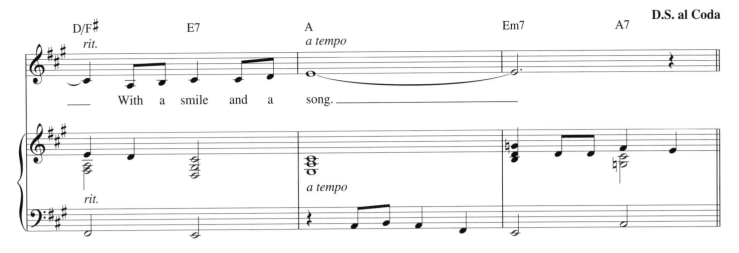

With a smile and a song.

CODA

fill the world with sun - shine. When you smile and you

sing, Ev - 'ry thing is in tune and it's spring and

life flows a - long, _____ With a smile and a song. _____

WHEN YOU WISH UPON A STAR

from Walt Disney's *Pinocchio*

Words by Ned Washington
Music by Leigh Harline

Anything your heart desires will come to you.

If your heart is in your dream, no request is too extreme,

When you wish upon a star as dreamers do.

Fate is kind, She brings to those who love,

the sweet ful - fill-ment of their se - cret long - ing.

Like a bolt out of the blue, Fate steps in and sees you through,

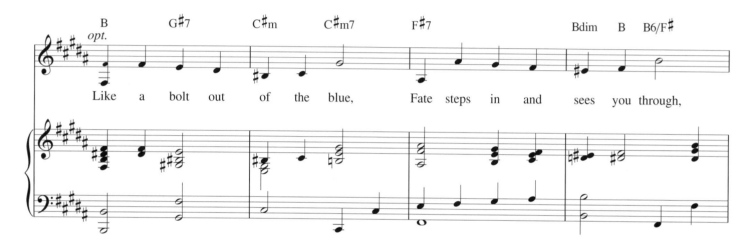

When you wish up - on a star your dream comes true.

Steadily

Fate is kind, She brings to those who love,

the sweet ful - fill-ment of their se-cret long - - - ing.

Like a bolt out of the blue, Fate steps in and

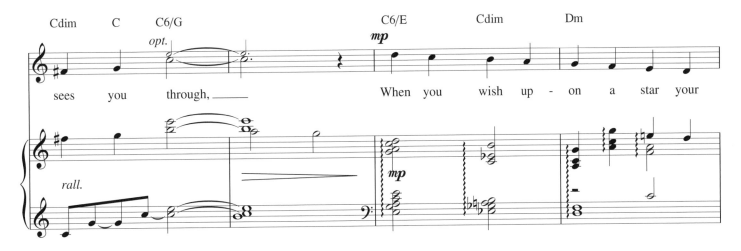

sees you through, _____ When you wish up - on a star your

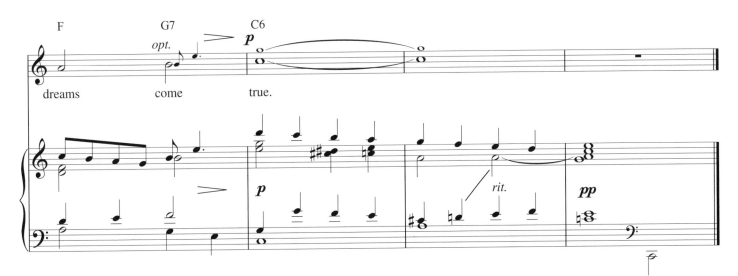

dreams come true.

ZIP-A-DEE-DOO-DAH
from Walt Disney's *Song Of the South*

Words by Ray Gilbert
Music by Allie Wrubel

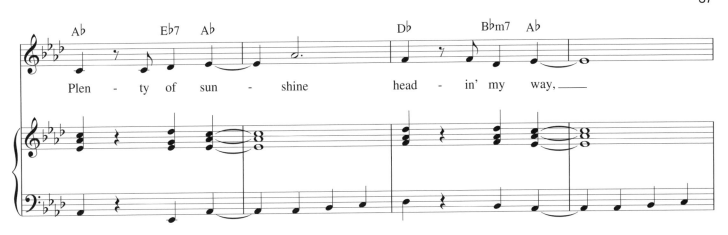

Plen - ty of sun - shine head - in' my way, _____

Zip - a - dee - doo - dah, zip - a - dee - ay! _____

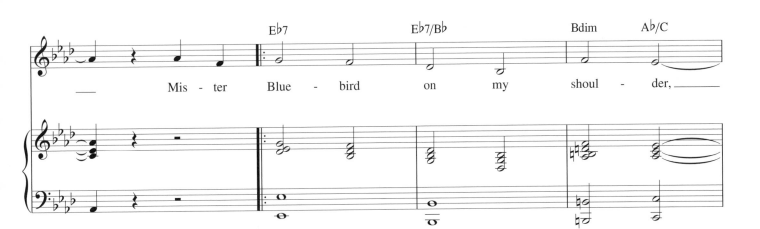

_____ Mis - ter Blue - bird on my shoul - der, _____

_____ it's the truth, it's "act - ch'll,"

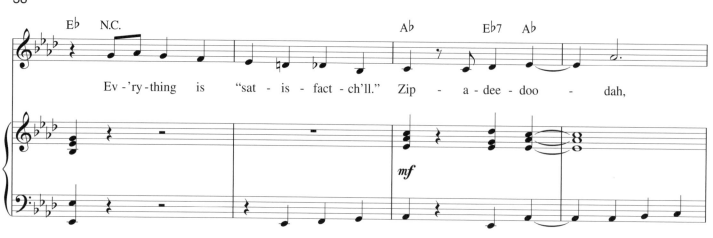

Ev -'ry-thing is "sat - is - fact - ch'll." Zip - a-dee-doo - dah,

zip - a - dee - ay! _____ Won - der - ful feel -

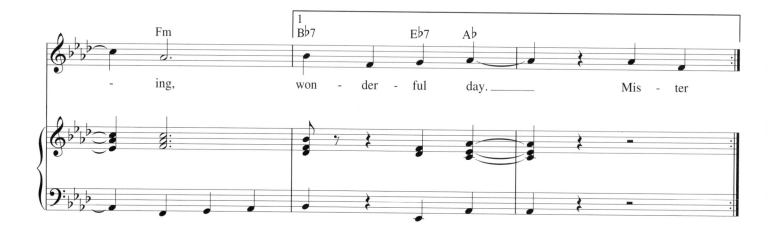

- ing, won - der - ful day. _____ Mis - ter

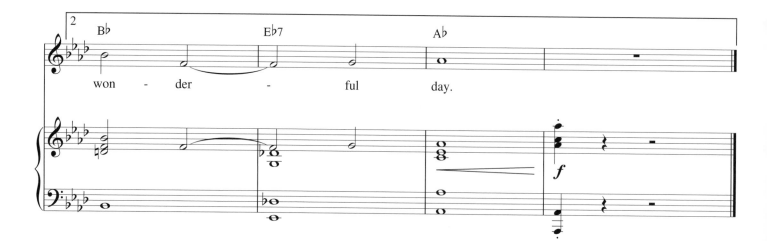

won - der - ful day.

About the Enhanced CD

In addition to full performances and piano accompaniments playable on both your CD player and computer, this enhanced CD also includes tempo adjustment and transposition software for computer use only. This software, known as the Amazing Slow Downer, was originally created for use in pop music to allow singers and players the freedom to independently adjust both tempo and pitch elements. Because we believe there may be valuable educational use for these features in classical and theatre music, we have included this software as a tool for both the teacher and student. For quick and easy installation instructions of this software please see below.

This new software feature allows you to adjust the tempo up and down without affecting the pitch. Likewise, the Amazing Slow Downer allows you to shift pitch up and down without affecting the tempo. We recommend that these new tempo and pitch adjustment features be used with care and insight. Ideally, you will be using these recorded accompaniments and the Amazing Slow Downer for practice only.

The audio quality may be somewhat compromised when played through the Amazing Slow Downer. This compromise in quality will not be a factor in playing the CD audio track on a normal CD player or through another audio computer program.

Installation instructions for the Amazing Slow Downer software:

For Macintosh OS 8, 9 and X:
- Load the CD-ROM into your CD-ROM Drive on your computer.
- Each computer is set up a little differently. Your computer may automatically open the audio CD portion of this enhanced CD and begin to play it.
- Double-click on the data portion of the CD-ROM (which will have the Hal Leonard icon in red and be named as the book).
- Double-click on the "Amazing OS 8 (9 or X)" folder.
- Double-click "Amazing Slow Downer"/"Amazing X PA" to run the software from the CD-ROM, or copy this file to your hard disk and run it from there.
- Follow the instructions on-screen to get started. The Amazing Slow Downer should display tempo, pitch and mix bars. Click to select your track and adjust pitch or tempo by sliding the appropriate bar to the left or to the right.

For Windows:
- Load the CD-ROM into your CD-ROM Drive on your computer.
- Each computer is set up a little differently. Your computer may automatically open the audio CD portion of this enhanced CD and begin to play it.
- To access the CD-ROM features, click on My Computer then right click on the Drive that you placed the CD in. Click Open. You should then see a folder named "Amazing Slow Downer". Click to open the "Amazing Slow Downer" folder.
- Double-click "setup.exe" to install the software from the CD-ROM to your hard disk. Follow the on-screen instructions to complete installation.
- Go to "Start", "Programs" and find the "Amazing Slow Downer" folder. Go to that folder and select the "Amazing Slow Downer" software.
- Follow the instructions on-screen to get started. The Amazing Slow Downer should display tempo, pitch and mix bars. Click to select your track and adjust pitch or tempo by sliding the appropriate bar to the left or to the right.
- Note: On Windows NT, 2000 and XP, the user should be logged in as the "Administrator" to guarantee access to the CD-ROM drive. Please see the help file for further information.

Minimum system requirements:

For Macintosh:
Power Macintosh; Mac OS 8.5 or higher; 4 MB Application RAM; 8x Multi-Session CD-ROM drive

For Windows:
Pentium Processor; Windows 95, 98, ME, NT, 2000, XP; 4 MB Application RAM; 8x Multi-Session CD-ROM drive